IMAGES
of America

AUBURN POLICE

On the cover: Please see page 17. (Author's collection.)

IMAGES
of America

AUBURN POLICE

Joseph E. DiVietro Jr.

ARCADIA
PUBLISHING

ISBN 978-0-7385-5035-0

Published by Arcadia Publishing
Charleston SC, Chicago IL, Portsmouth NH, San Francisco CA

Printed in the United States of America

Library of Congress Catalog Card Number: 2007922177

For all general information contact Arcadia Publishing at:
Telephone 843-853-2070
Fax 843-853-0044
E-mail sales@arcadiapublishing.com
For customer service and orders:
Toll-Free 1-888-313-2665

Visit us on the Internet at www.arcadiapublishing.com

In memory of my grandparents,
Marion and Joseph "Herky" DiVietro
and Mary and Ted Bouck.

Contents

ACKNOWLEDGMENTS

This project would not have been possible if so many people had not donated their family photographs, given their stories of past events, and shared their memories of loved ones. Auburn police officer Tom Weed is the historian for the police department. His insight into past events and his ability to name the persons and places pictured were a tremendous help. Special thanks go to Sheila Tucker of the Cayuga County historian's office and to Jack Cavanaugh of Cavanaugh Studio of Photography on South Street for his help in bringing old negatives back to life. Thanks also go to Pam O'Neil, my editor at Arcadia Publishing, for guiding me through the book-building process.

INTRODUCTION

On April 11, 1848, at the second meeting of the common council of the newly formed City of Auburn, the mayor submitted a list of standing committees. On this list was the Committee on Police and Licenses. Its first members were Shubail Cottle, Charles Coffin, and Edward Barber. The following month the committee hired Jacob Sheiver as constable.

In November 1848, the Watch and Lamp District was created. A position of city marshal was also put into effect. The marshal, by city ordinance definition, was to aid the mayor in faithful execution of the bylaws and ordinances of the city. The captain of the Watch and Lamp District was authorized to fix the time of duty and the number of watchmen to be employed. An amendment was also added that said all individuals appointed watchmen also be appointed special constables.

By 1855, the city had a justice of the peace, city marshal, and constables. In May 1858, a petition from city marshal Joseph White asked to hire a special policeman at $1.25 a day. The motion passed, and the city had its first policeman. In 1869, the charter was changed to read that the mayor could appoint up to 12 policemen.

The Committee on Police and Licenses was replaced by the Board of Charities and Police in 1879. The new board was made up of the mayor and commissioners. John Underwood was the first chairman. The board was authorized to hire up to 20 policemen and as many special policemen without pay as deemed necessary. The board also appointed a chief of police and a captain of police with fixed salaries.

In 1879, C. W. Jennings was appointed chief of police. Jennings's men were inspected prior to coming on duty every day. The inspections took place at the armory. Jennings was responsible for the new badges that resembled a shield. Each badge was inscribed "Auburn Police." New hats were also worn. The hats were the helmet type that were worn by the New York Metropolitan Police. Jennings resigned in 1882 because, as he said, the commissioners had ignored every applicant he had recommended for the position on the force.

Henry D. Crosbie became chief. Crosbie had been appointed to the force in 1879 by Mayor Osborne. He died on the job in 1889. His obituary said of him that "He knew every crook in the city and took pains to keep an eye on them."

On August 20, 1884, Charles E. MacMaster, age 32, was appointed police officer for the city of Auburn. In June 1892, MacMaster was named chief of police. The new chief oversaw 17 patrolmen: Benjamin B. Roseboom, George Fullmer, Thomas O. Shaw, Arthur Titus, John A. McCarthy, Patrick Graney, Edward Holmes, Edger Boynton, John Woodall, James Malone, Norman Parker, Jesse Atwater, Thomas Hickey, Robert Breese, Charles Gill, John Anton, and David Schute. There were three supervisors. Frederick J. Nash was the police commissioner.

During MacMaster's term, the eight-hour shift system was put in place, giving the city police protection at all hours. Auburn was the first city in the state of comparable size to integrate the eight-hour shift for around-the-clock protection. MacMaster served as chief for 11 years. In his 11th year, he was reassigned as a patrolman by the new administration at city hall. At the time, patrolman were generally forced out with the change of mayors at city hall. The retiring mayor took his policemen with him.

The monthly payroll for the entire department was $1,847. MacMaster spent 35 years on the force. MacMaster's last report to city hall for the month of December 1903 showed the department making 100 arrests, 93 being males; fines of $169 were collected; two patrolmen called in sick; 38 doors were found open; 87 people received lodging at the police department; 11 complains were made by citizens; and four reports were filed by police officers.

In January 1904, William C. Bell, age 34, was appointed the next chief of police. The appointment came under the administration of Thomas Mott Osborne. Bell served for 27 years before dying on the job from appendicitis.

Capt. Edward Holmes was appointed acting chief. Holmes was appointed to the department in 1892. He served on the department for 37 years, before retiring under Mayor Charles Osborne. Holmes received a $1,440-a-year pension.

Chester John Bills was appointed the next chief of police by city manager John F. Donovan on April 1, 1929. At the time of his appointment, Bills was superintendent of supplies at Auburn prison. He was a former police officer and veteran of World War I, serving in France in the 108th infantry. Bills retired in 1953.

In August 1953, John F. Tenity took over as chief when Bills retired. Tenity was appointed patrolman on April 1, 1922, by city manager John P. Jaeckel. After two years he was assigned to motorcycle duty, and in 1931, he was given a patrol car. Tenity was appointed sergeant by city manager Arthur Adams in 1941. Six years later, in 1947, he was promoted to captain by city manager George B. Train. The new chief had a son on the force, Francis J. Tenity.

John T. Costello took over as chief in 1959. Costello was promoted by city manager George F. Train. Costello served in the U.S. Navy in the mid-1940s. He was a graduate of the FBI Academy. He joined the department in June 1950. Costello was promoted to sergeant in 1955 and to captain in 1957. As captain he made $4,800 a year. As chief he made $5,700.

When Costello retired in 1988, Assistant Chief John C. Walter was named interim chief. Later, city manager Bruce Clifford appointed Walter permanent chief of police. At the time of his appointment, Walter was a 17-year veteran of the department, having been appointed to it in 1970. He went through the ranks in the patrol division and was promoted to sergeant by Costello in 1974. Walter retired in 1991.

John Ecklund took over as chief in 1992. He was one of the only chiefs appointed in Auburn that had no Auburn ties and no service with the department. Originally from Jamestown, Ecklund had a short career in Auburn. He retired in 1995 and left town shortly thereafter.

In 1996, the current chief, Gary Giannotta, was appointed to the position of chief of police. Appointed to the department in 1981, Giannotta was promoted to sergeant in 1988 and to captain in 1990 by city manger Bruce Clifford. The current Auburn Police Department has 72 sworn officers. There are several specialized units in the department, including school recourse officers, community police officers, a DWI (Driving While Intoxicated) patrol, and a commercial vehicle enforcement unit.

At its inception and up until 1930, the department offices were in city hall at the corner of North and Franklin Streets. In 1930, the old city hall was taken down and the current police department was built in its place, at 46 North Street. The building's exterior appearance has remained mostly unchanged since the 1930s.

Much of the interior, however, has changed over the years. The building still houses a cell block with eight male cells and two female cells. Each cell has a sink, toilet, and wooden plank to sit or sleep on. The building once housed a shooting range in the basement. That area has since been converted to a weight room. Weapons qualifications are now done at an outside location.

The building was constructed with a three-car garage. In the late 1980s, the garage was converted to offices for the desk sergeant, patrol captain, and switchboard operator. The operator also acted as a police dispatcher. The police department no longer has a switchboard operator. All calls coming into the police department are answered by the 911 center at the sheriff's department. The 911 center also dispatches all calls for service.

Auburn City Court had its courtroom on the first floor of the police department until moving into the old post office building on Genesee Street. The area left vacated by city court was converted to what is now called Records. This is a unit consisting of civilians who have the responsibility of storing and maintaining all police documents. The remainder of the first floor is administrative offices.

The second floor is the current home of the Detective and Identification Bureaus. At one time all photographs taken by the department were developed in a second-floor dark room. That room now houses computer-related equipment. All film development is done by a private company. Call boxes scattered throughout the city have been replaced by computers in the cars that can access data from local and state records in seconds.

The police department, with more than 150 years of serving the community, has a history that deserves to be preserved. The images in *Auburn Police*, forgotten by most, offer a glimpse of many of the men and women who have been part of that history.

One

Chiefs of Police

William C. Bell served as police chief from 1904 to 1929. On November 1, 1901, Bell, or "Billie" as his friends called him, was appointed to the police department. Under the administration of Thomas Mott Osborne, Bell was appointed police chief on February 1, 1904. Bell succeeded Chief Charles E. MacMaster.

Chester John Bills was police chief from 1929 to 1953, succeeding Chief William Bell. A lifelong resident of Auburn, Bills was born on March 25, 1893. During World War I, he served in France in the 108th Infantry. Prior to being appointed police chief, Bills was the superintendent of supplies at the Auburn prison.

John F. Tenity was chief from 1953 to 1959. He took over as acting chief after the retirement of Bills. Then, in August 1953, city manager Alfred Turner made the appointment permanent. Three other police captains—Robert Riley, Joseph Conboy, and Raymond Donovan—were vying for the job.

John T. Costello served as chief from 1959 to 1988. Born on July 7, 1927, he was a lifelong resident of Auburn. He graduated from the FBI Academy in Washington, D.C., and served in the U.S. Navy. He was appointed police chief, earning $5,700 a year, by city manager George F. Train.

John C. Walter was chief from 1988 to 1991. He joined the force in November 1970 and became sergeant in April 1974, captain in December 1979, and assistant chief of police on August 5, 1987.

John Ecklund served as chief from 1992 to 1995. Originally from Jamestown, he moved to Auburn after being appointed chief. He was one of the few "outsiders" to make the rank of Auburn police chief. He resigned from the position in 1995 and left town shortly thereafter.

Gary Giannotta (center) was promoted to chief on January 22, 1996. Hired by the department in 1981, he was promoted to sergeant in 1988 and to captain in 1990. Assistant Fire Chief Bob Sloan is on the right.

Two

OFFICERS ON DUTY

In full-dress uniform, the officers stand on the steps of the old city hall on May 10, 1914. Police chief William Bell (front, wearing a suit and tie) is flanked by his two captains.

A sergeant leads 11 Auburn police officers in a parade through town in the early 1900s. At one time the police department marched in parades in full-dress uniform.

Officer Wesley Bunnell directs traffic in 1910. Bunnell was appointed to the force on June 19, 1904. While on foot patrol in July 1906, he apprehended Joseph Ravana, who had just stabbed a woman on Water Street. During the arrest Ravana cut Bunnell in the back with the same knife that was used in the assault against the woman.

This officer is on an Indian motorcycle. The first Indian motorcycles rolled out of the factory in 1902, so this is probably one of the first motorized bikes used by the department. This 1910 photograph was taken in front of the old city hall on Market Street.

Auburn's first paddy wagon is pictured in August 1919. The officer standing on the back of the wagon is wearing the metropolitan-style hat originally commissioned by police chief C. W. Jennings in 1879. "City of Auburn" can be seen painted on the front of the wagon.

Veteran members of Auburn's finest are seen here. The officer's are standing on the front steps of the old city hall. The officer third from the left is a sergeant, he is wearing a "newer" style of badge that is still in use today.

The armory is pictured in 1910. Prior to coming on duty, every officer had to be inspected for appearance. The original state armory was on Water Street near State Street.

This officer poses with a newer model Indian motorcycle on Genesee Street around 1915. Notice the second seat on the bike. The building on the left is now Gregory and Picciano Electric. The building on the right is gone, and today the Dunkin' Donuts is on that site.

Officer Albert Green was promoted to sergeant, with a salary of $1,300 a year, in May 1919. He and officer Daniel Randall were promoted to sergeant at the same time by police commissioner Edger S. Jennings.

Leo B. Lightfoot was the first African American appointed to the police force. Lightfoot was appointed on May 2, 1881. On his first night on duty, 200 people gathered at city hall to see Lightfoot march out for duty after taking his oath and receiving instructions from Chief Underwood.

Beecher Flummerfelt (in uniform) stands behind a brand-new Blitz Buggy. The police department took delivery of the Indian three-wheeled dispatch tow on September 6, 1941. The motorcycle was put in service enforcing the new two-hour parking limits in North and Northwest Auburn.

Henry Mitchell was appointed to the police department on September 24, 1927. In November 1947, he was promoted to sergeant and served as head of security for the National Bank of Auburn. In 1950, he was awarded a gold trophy for winning first place in the New York State indoor pistol matches at the IBM grounds in Endicott. Mitchell retired on April 1, 1953.

Joseph Falcone was appointed to the police department on August 15, 1913. He was promoted to sergeant in 1932 and to detective sergeant in 1936. He was the first person of Italian descent to be hired by the police department. His great nephew Joseph DiVietro is a police sergeant on the force today.

Two detectives use an original Teletype machine. The Teletype system is still used today by almost all police agencies in the country to send other agencies messages regarding missing persons, wanted persons, and other information.

A command officer mans an original dispatching system. When the police department purchased a system for dispatching calls to officers in the field, very few cars and no foot patrolmen had radios.

This is an original wanted poster for Sebastian Trusso. Trusso shot and killed Gaetano Salva the morning of September 8, 1913. This poster was mailed to area police agencies.

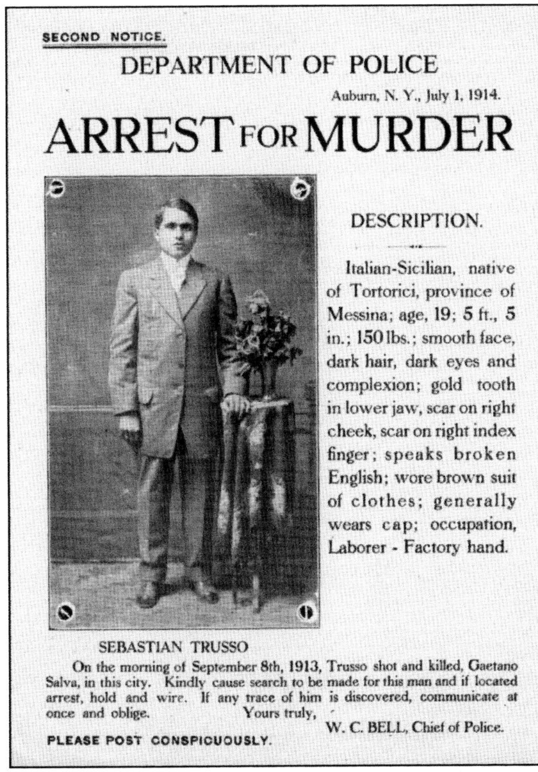

SECOND NOTICE.

DEPARTMENT OF POLICE

Auburn, N. Y., July 1, 1914.

ARREST FOR MURDER

DESCRIPTION.

Italian-Sicilian, native of Tortorici, province of Messina; age, 19; 5 ft., 5 in.; 150 lbs.; smooth face, dark hair, dark eyes and complexion; gold tooth in lower jaw, scar on right cheek, scar on right index finger; speaks broken English; wore brown suit of clothes; generally wears cap; occupation, Laborer - Factory hand.

SEBASTIAN TRUSSO

On the morning of September 8th, 1913, Trusso shot and killed, Gaetano Salva, in this city. Kindly cause search to be made for this man and if located arrest, hold and wire. If any trace of him is discovered, communicate at once and oblige.

Yours truly,

W. C. BELL, Chief of Police.

PLEASE POST CONSPICUOUSLY.

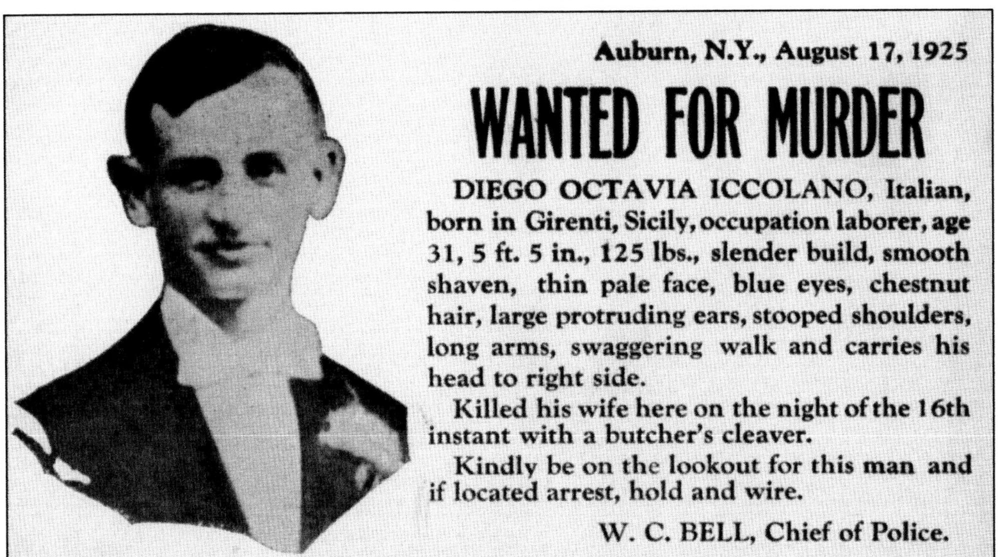

Auburn, N.Y., August 17, 1925

WANTED FOR MURDER

DIEGO OCTAVIA ICCOLANO, Italian, born in Girenti, Sicily, occupation laborer, age 31, 5 ft. 5 in., 125 lbs., slender build, smooth shaven, thin pale face, blue eyes, chestnut hair, large protruding ears, stooped shoulders, long arms, swaggering walk and carries his head to right side.

Killed his wife here on the night of the 16th instant with a butcher's cleaver.

Kindly be on the lookout for this man and if located arrest, hold and wire.

W. C. BELL, Chief of Police.

This is an original wanted poster. Diego Octavia Iccolano killed his wife Josephine at 38 South Division Street the night of August 17, 1925. Police questioned all of Iccolano's relatives and neighbors. When Iccolano could not be located he was listed as a fugitive from justice. Police began a larger search and flyers were sent to all New York State Police agencies and to Italian Consulates. Particular attention was paid to seaports in New York, Philadelphia, and Boston. As time passed, information developed that Iccolano had either made his was to Italy or was trying to do so. He was never found.

Officers pose for a group photograph. From left to right are (first row) civilian Clayton Bell, Lawrence (Larry) Mentillo, Davis Catalano, Paul Clancy, civilian Bill Simons, Leo Flynn, Robert Orman, and Raymond Donovan; (second row) ? Fogarty, Carlos Nicandri, Joseph Conboy, Sam Emmi, Hugh Casey, Hank Chyka, John Sawran, Sam Testa, and Vitto Tozzi; (third row) Francis Tenity, John Doyle, Clarence Vatter, Frank Colella, Michael Breanick, John Walsh, Michael Tartaglia, Wayne Armitage, Carmen Bertonica, John Walawender, and Earl Moochler.

All six of these officers were appointed to the department in 1929. From left to right are (first row) Joseph Ryan (made sergeant in November 1947), Pete Namisnak, and Art Reilly (captain). The second row includes Joseph Fogarty (made sergeant in November 1950) and Joseph Myers.

Inspector detective Larry Mentillo (front left) is pictured at the corner of Genesee and Market Streets in the 1950s with a uniformed officer. The old Flat Iron Building (right background) is a park today, and the site behind Mentillo is now occupied by Dunkin' Donuts.

Five officers are pictured with police vehicles outside the station. From left to right are (first row) Michael Tartaglia and Robert Oropallo; (second row) Vito Tozzi (appointed patrolman on July 26, 1952; retired on July 10, 1977), unidentified, and Danny DeMaio.

Standing by their police vehicles are, from left to right, officers John Tenity, Carl Moochler, William Dowski, and Doyle Wenner. Appointed patrolman on July 1, 1948, Dowski retired in March 1972. Moochler, who retired in 1973, was appointed patrolman in January 1948, assistant identification officer in October 1953, and identification officer in August 1965.

William L. Simmonds investigates a safe job. Simmonds joined the department on July 1, 1937. Two years later he was appointed fingerprint operator and photographer. During his career, he was responsible for classifying over 50,000 fingerprints. In April 1938, he gained national recognition for getting a fingerprint off paper that was found inside a safe. The safe had been broken into at the Jefferson Theatre on State Street.

Lined up in the late 1950s are, from left to right, officers John Costello, Wayne Armitage, Hank Myers, Michael Breanick (standing in back), Anthony Longo, Davis Catalano, Michael Tartaglia, and Charlie DeChick. Breanick, a U.S. Army veteran, was appointed on July 1, 1950, and was promoted to sergeant on May 1, 1956.

Every summer the department holds a clambake. Eating corn at the annual event are, from left to right, (first row) unidentified and Doyle Wenner; (second row) Walter Wallawender, Joseph Conboy, Peter Namisnak, and Leo Flynn.

Posing for a photograph in December 1954 are, from left to right, (first row) Wayne Armitage, John Costello, and Sam Testa; (second row) Davis Catalano and Frank Colella.

With the calendar behind them showing April 1955, the officers are, from left to right, (first row) Pete Namisnak and Michael Tartaglia; (second row) Clarence Vatter, John Costello, and Sam Testa.

Officers of the Police Benevolent Association are, from left to right, Michael Tartaglia, Sam Testa, Frank Colella, and Carmen Bertonica. The police department still has a Police Benevolent Association, but all contractual issues are handled by the police union, a separate entity.

A motor vehicle accident occurred on Grant Avenue. Officer Vito Tozzi (in uniform) is behind the police car on the left, and photographer Andy Tarby is in the middle of the road, not far from Tozzi. Today, on the right, the large field is occupied by Auburn Plaza and Self Service Gas is a Hess gas station.

Carrying their nightsticks are, from left to right, officers Carl Nicandri, Robert Randall, John Costello, and John Kozial. Randall, a U.S. Navy veteran, was appointed to the department on May 15, 1950. Costello went on to be chief of police. Kozial, a military veteran, became a patrolman in November 1952 and resigned in 1952 for an appointment to the postal service.

Identification officer William Simmonds fingerprints George Sawyer on November 23, 1960. The identification officer took all fingerprints on the second floor of the police station. Today the officer making the arrest fingerprints the prisoner using a "live scan" machine that electronically sends the prints to Albany for comparisons. Simmonds, after serving in the fingerprinting department since 1937, retired in 1965 at the age of 70 and died one year later.

Wayne Armitage rides a Harley-Davidson motorcycle. Armitage was appointed patrolman on October 1, 1949, and was assigned to the traffic squad on July 3, 1950. He made the rank of detective in May 1956, sergeant on January 11, 1959, captain on May 1, 1968, and captain of the detectives on February 1, 1985. He retired in 1987, after 38 years of service. Today his daughter, Marilyn Kelley, is a civilian working at the police department's Identification Bureau.

From left to right are (first row) Henry Mitchell, unidentified, John Chayka (appointed patrolman June 15, 1923), and officer Brandstetter; (second row) unidentified, Larry Mentillo, unidentified, Pete Namisnak, two unidentified men, and Frank Colella. Chayka was appointed a patrolman on June 15, 1923.

This station wagon was involved in a hit-and-run accident on Grant Avenue in 1967. Capt. Beecher Flummerfelt took this photograph inside the police garage on October 29 of that year. At that time there was a three-car garage attached to the police building. The garage has since been converted to office space.

Officer Charlie Gummerson (left) and Ron Semple have traffic duty downtown in front of the Auburn Savings Bank on July 17, 1967. Gummerson was appointed on May 14, 1961. Semple, who retired in 1997, became a patrolman on July 1, 1962, and later, traffic officer in charge of maintaining the department's fleet of cars.

An accident reconstruction class is held at the intersection of Willard and Dexter Streets. From left to right are unidentified, Beecher Flummerfelt, Charlie DeChick, Bill Dowski, John Worbick, Charlie Elser Sr., Harold Quinn, Syracuse chief Frank Sardino (squatting), Edward Burkhardt, unidentified, Davis Catalono, Dom DeSocio (squatting), Robert Oropollo, John Costello, Robert Orman, and Joe Conboy.

Officer Robert Oropollo investigates a car accident on Parker Street. He is leaning on the back of a 1961 Chevrolet Impala cruiser. His motorcycle is seen in the right foreground. Born on April 15, 1924, Oropollo was appointed patrolman on November 24, 1947.

Walking beats were a large part of police work up to the 1980s. There were eight walking beats in the 1950s and three in the 1970s—posts 1, 2, and 3. Officers assigned a walking beat did not carry a portable radio. They had to ring a call box every half hour or a sergeant would go out looking for them. There were 18 call boxes in and around downtown. Pictured in front of Auburn Tobacco Company on their walking beat are officers Carl Townsend (left) and Raymond Wood.

In July 1959, officer Robert Oropollo was on his motorcycle waiting for a signal light at Genesee and Fulton Streets when a station wagon behind him started up as the light changed. The station wagon, operated by George Ward of 162 Genesee Street, rear-ended the motorcycle, knocking it over and sending Oropollo to the ground. Oropollo was uninjured. The bike, however, sprang a leak in the engine.

Officer Sam Testa shows a bicycle that was involved in a motor vehicle accident. In the 1960s photograph, taken in the police garage, Testa is wearing a white summer uniform shirt. Dark blue shirts were worn in the winter. Today officers wear a standard dark blue shirt all year.

An automobile accident occurred in front of 180 East Genesee Street on May 27, 1961. Officer John Malandruccolo stands next to the 1959 Chevrolet patrol car. Malandruccolo was appointed patrolman on August 22, 1968, by city manager Alfred Turner and was promoted to detective on September 16, 1968. He retired on November 15, 1987. Sgt. Edward Burkhardt took this photograph.

Officer Carl Nicandri points to evidence in the road. Appointed patrolman on May 15, 1950, Nicandri retired on January 1, 1976. Notice in many of the pictures it was common practice for the officer to point to the item being photographed.

Officer John Malandruccolo investigates a burglary at Piccalo Sales on July 15, 1964. Piccalo Sales, a wholesale distributor of groceries, was located at 27 Clark Street. Sgt. Edward Burkhardt took the photograph.

Burkhardt investigates a hit-and-run accident that occurred at 1 East Genesee Street on February 27, 1964. The car belonged to Lester Walters. Burkhardt, a World War II veteran, was appointed patrolman on July 1, 1950. He was promoted to sergeant in 1959 and to captain on July 3, 1966.

State senator George Metcalf (right) meets with three officers on May 28, 1962. Metcalf was elected to the state senate in 1950. During his 15 years in the legislature, he authored many bills in the area of fair housing, civil rights, and public health. Between 1980 and 1988, he was board chairman of the Columbian Rope company. With him from left to right are Sam Testa, Carl Festa, and Dom DeSocio.

Members of the dance committee meet on May 6, 1959, to discuss plans for the policeman's ball. From left to right are (first row) Carl Nicandri, Michael Tartaglia, Walt Walawender, and Carmen Bertonica; (second row) Sam Testa, Frank Colella, Clarence Vatter, and Vito Tozzi. Colella was appointed patrolman on May 20, 1953, and was promoted to sergeant on June 1, 1969; he retired in 1988. Vatter was appointed patrolman on October 22, 1934.

Gen. Alexander Ismodes (left), chief of the Peru police, visits Auburn on May 29, 1958. With him are, from left to right, his interpreter, Joe Cuddy, Chief John Tenity, and a city official.

Officer Dom DeSocio points to a door that was pried open in a burglary. DeSocio was appointed patrolman on March 15, 1955, by city manager Alfred Turner. He retired on June 22, 1980, and died one year later.

At a presentation on February 28, 1962, are, from left to right, Sam Testa, Vito Tozzi, Steve Emmi, Davis Catalano, Jimmy Cioffa, and Leo Pinckney. Cioffa was appointed patrolman on June 6, 1960, and was promoted to detective on January 1, 1971. He retired on December 4, 1987.

The "sound car" is pictured on November 30, 1955. The vehicle was called the sound car because it was equipped with a two-way radio, allowing the officer in the car to speak with police headquarters. Not all cars had radios during this time, and no one on the walking beat had a radio. Shown are Robert Oropallo (left) and Robert Orman.

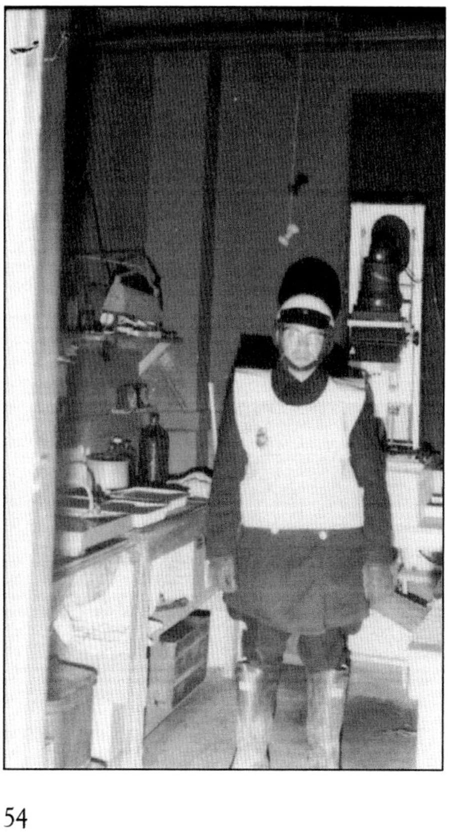

Sam Italiano pauses for a photograph while developing film in the darkroom on the second floor of the police department. In 2001, the darkroom equipment was auctioned off to make way for computer servers used by the department. Italiano was appointed patrolman on November 6, 1972, and was later promoted to assistant identification officer and then to identification officer on August 15, 1974. He retired on February 9, 1990.

Officers John Loveland (left) and Carl Festa were members of the traffic squad. Four officers were assigned to the unit in the early 1960s. Their job was to direct traffic at three intersections: William and Genesee Streets, State and Genesee Streets, and North and Genesee Streets. Loveland was appointed patrolman on March 2, 1953, and was promoted to sergeant on July 3, 1966. He retired in June 1988.

Officer Michael Tartaglia (left) and Captain Reilly stand in the courtroom at the police department on January 22, 1959. Up until the late 1970s, city court was held at the police department. When the state took over the court system, city court was moved to its current home, at the old post office building downtown. Today this room is used as the records office.

Some things never change. The police garage is full of bicycles on June 2, 1972. Today the police garage is still full of bicycles—all found on city streets and turned in to the police department. Twice a year the department holds an event to auction off the bicycles.

At the scene of a burglary are, from left to right, (first row) unidentified and identification officer William Simmonds; (second row) officers John Sawran and John Worobick. Appointed patrolman on August 7, 1950, Worobick was assigned motorcycle duty in September 1950. In September 1951, he broke two bones after he was hit by a car while riding the police motorcycle at the intersection of Genesee and Osborne Streets.

Officer Peter Namisnak is pictured in November 1951. He succeeded officer Clair Stanton and became president of the Police Benevolent Association that included the Seneca Falls and Waterloo Police Departments.

Officer John Matthews (left) was chasing a vehicle when his patrol car crashed into the guardrail by 84 Lumber. With him is Sam Emmi. Matthews, who was appointed patrolman on July 1, 1962, retired in 1975.

Yes, a Ford Pinto was a police car. This 1973 model was used on the downtown beat. It is parked on Market Street in front of the police department. Today this area is a parking lot for the patrol cars. Notice the buildings in the background. The Marine Midland Bank building (left) is all that survived urban renewal.

Officer Sam Testa points to the cracked windshield of a 1957 taxicab, the result of the vehicle having hit a bicyclist. Notice the chalk drawing on the roadway. The picture dates from the early 1960s.

In 1976, the Plymouth Fury was the choice for police cars. These cars were painted light blue and white to celebrate the bicentennial year. A special shirt badge was issued that year, replacing the metal badge. At the end of the year the officers went back to the traditional metal badges. From left to right are Sgt. Michael Breanick and officers Dan DeMaio, Dom DeSocio, Tom Weed, and Tom Burger.

Officer John Malandruccolo investigates a car accident. Malandruccolo was appointed patrolman on August 22, 1955, and was promoted to detective in 1968. He retired in 1987. He and others were honored in 1988 for service to the community at a dinner arranged by assemblyman Michael Nozzolio at Springside Inn.

Target practice is held at the Cayuga County Sportsmen's Club on Rockefeller Road. Among the officers pictured are Robert Randall, Beecher Flummerfelt, Carl Festa, Dom DeSocio, Charlie DeChick, and Vito Tozzi. Today every officer has to qualify with his or her service weapon twice a year. This includes using the shotgun.

Pictured in October 1976 are officer Pete Killian (left) and detective Carl Festa (right). A U.S. Air Force veteran, Festa was appointed patrolman on June 1, 1956, was promoted to detective on January 6, 1971, and, in 1983, was named Man of the Year by the Christopher Columbus Commemorative Committee and Auburn Lodge 2368 for his community service. He retired after a 32-year career.

Police investigate a motor vehicle accident on the corner of Seymour Street at North Street on March 6, 1979. Accidents still occur on a regular basis at this intersection. The patrol cars are Chevrolet Novas. The Super-Duper (right) is now gone, and the site is currently occupied by a video store and tanning salon.

This Chevrolet Nova was involved in an accident of its own. The design of the patrol cars was pretty simple in the early 1970s: a seal on the door, with the department phone number and police written on the back trunk area. The vehicle is parked at the police department.

This 1963 Ford Fairlane patrol car got sideswiped. The car is parked on Market Street next to the police department. The hood and trunk area were painted blue on these patrol cars. In the background, the building with the four overhead doors is the fire department's headquarters.

An officer points to damage sustained by a car in an accident on a snowy night in the late 1950s or early 1960s. His long coat is a style that the department no longer uses. The photograph was taken in front of the New Yorker restaurant, located on Genesee Street, across from Hunter's Diner. All of the buildings on the right are now gone.

Officer Pete Aversa (left) stands at the intersection of Genesee and Fulton Streets. The cars are parked in the parking lot of Homicks repair station. The repair station was knocked down to make way for a chain drugstore in the 1990s. Aversa was appointed patrolman on October 3, 1965, at the age of 28. He retired on April 6, 1979.

The Plymouth (left) owned by Joseph R. Leana of Cameron Street was stolen on August 17, 1963, in front of Hunter's Diner on Genesee Street. State police in Ithaca found the car badly damaged in a state parking area. Sgt. Edward Burkhardt took this photograph on September 13, 1963.

Officers get ready to deliver Christmas baskets to needy families in December 1960. Today the police union still delivers food and other items to needy families around the holiday season. Although the baskets no longer look like these, the deliveries continue to be a much-needed help to families.

Officer Robert Oropollo is standing next to a 1961 Chevrolet on the corner of South and Exchange Streets. The Chevrolet hit and injured officer Jimmy Cioffa while Cioffa was standing in the road. Cioffa later returned to work and did not retire until 1987.

Capt. Hugh Casey smiles on his last day of work, January 2, 1985. Casey was appointed to the department on November 24, 1947. In June 1952, he spent time in the Detective Bureau as acting detective and then returned to patrol the following month. He was promoted to sergeant in December 1955 and to captain in May 1969.

Officer Tom Burger was driving this Plymouth Fury down Seymour Street toward State Street in late 1970 when a car made a right-hand turn onto Seymour Street, cutting Burger off. Attempting to stop the car, Burger made it to Seymour Street at Washington Street before his patrol car hit a patch of ice. The end result is pictured. Burger was not injured in the accident, and the other car was never found. When a patrol car gets into an accident, someone has to tell the chief. An accident like this one is best told over the telephone.

These youngsters were pulled out of the Owasco Outlet near the prison. Officer Carl Festa (right) and his follow officers are wearing white summer shirts. A short time after this photograph was taken, the department switched to light blue shirts for patrolman and white shirts for command staff. The same color was worn all year. In the early 1990s, the switch was made to dark blue shirts for the entire department.

Officers Carl Festa (left) and Sam Emmi look over recovered evidence. Emmi has a long family history at the department. His brother Steve was a patrolman; his father-in-law, Larry Mentillo, retired as a detective; and his son, Daniel, is a police captain with the department today.

This 1972 Chevrolet Bel Air patrol car is parked at the police department. Notice the number one sticker near the back door. Until the mid-1990s, all of the cars had a single car number: car 1, car 2, and so on. After that the car numbers were changed to three digits. Today car 1 would be unit 411.

Motorcycle officers Moochler (left) and John Tenity stand together in uniform. The motorcycle officer's uniform always stood out with its high boots and motorcycle pants. Of course, the roar of the Harley-Davidson motorcycle engine announced the arrival of the police.

The three-wheeled Cushmans were used downtown to check parking meters, along with regular patrol functions. In 1971, officer Robert Oropollo turned this Cushman over on Genesee Street. As a result of injuries he sustained in the accident, Oropollo was never able to return to work.

In 1972, officer Tony Longo (back right) ran for the school board. To gain publicity, Longo, along with several other officers, joined a parade. Pictured with Longo are officers Dan Colella and Leo Tortorici (foreground), and Mike Cicora and James Cioffa (center).

This is one of the eight men's cells in the police department. The women have two cells identical to this one. The cells have changed very little since the police station was built. Metal toilets and sinks have replaced porcelain units, which were constantly being broken by prisoners. The cells are four feet wide by eight feet long, and the wooden plank is all that is provided—there are no pillows or mattresses. A blanket is provided only if the prisoner asks for one. Breakfast is black coffee and toast.

Officers Allan Wilson (left) and Dan Colella show off an award they won in a shooting competition. Wilson, a Vietnam War veteran, was appointed to the department on July 23, 1973. He was promoted to sergeant on February 1, 1985, and to captain on October 5, 1987. While captain, he served in several areas: patrol, training office, and captain in charge of the Detective Bureau.

A team searches for a young woman who disappeared in Auburn on September 28, 1981. The body of Julie Monson, 18, was later recovered in a swamp in the area. Officers are, from left to right, Don Quinn, Harold "Red" Quinn, Carl Festa, Dick Noga, and Charlie Elser.

Officer Charles Elser Sr. investigates a car accident on Osborne Street. In November 1966, Elser was assigned to the Identification Bureau as an identification officer. His annual salary for the new position was the same as that of a patrolman: $5,616. Elser's two sons went into careers in law enforcement; Charles Elser Jr. retired a patrolman from the Auburn Police Department, and Bobby Elser retired a sergeant from the Syracuse Police Department.

Officer Sam Emmi (right) investigates a car accident involving a city truck near Hoopes Park in early 1960. In 1974, Emmi was sworn in as court interpreter. A man named Michael Moscatelli was charged with assault and was about to stand trial. Moscatelli only spoke about 25 percent English and needed an Italian translator. Officer Emmi acted as the translator.

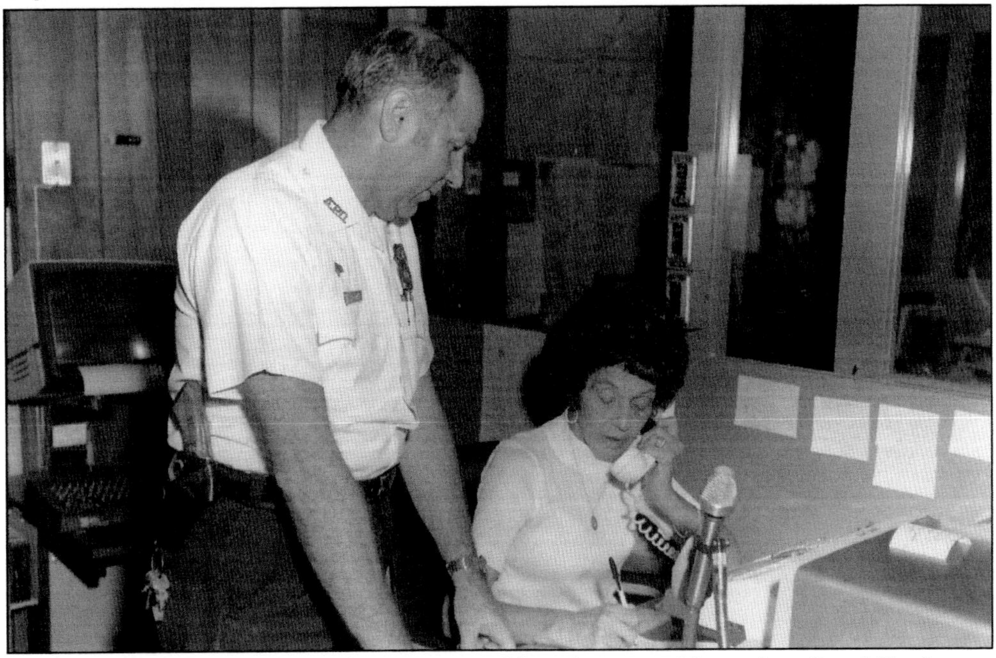

Capt. Edward L. Burkhardt stands next to switchboard operator Norma Jean Randall, who was appointed switchboard operator on January 25, 1971. The photograph was taken in the old communications room in the early 1970s. After the three-car garage attached to the police building was converted to offices, the communications room was moved to that space.

Officers take inventory of seized evidence: drugs that were taken from Lewis's drugstore at the five points. From left to right are detective Carl Festa, Chief John Costello, and detective Harold "Red" Quinn. Quinn was appointed patrolman on June 2, 1954, by city manager Alfred Turner and was promoted to detective on July 6, 1983.

The Onondaga County sheriff's department helicopter has landed in the parking lot at the Holiday Inn. Detectives used the helicopter to search the area around the college for missing 18-year-old Julie Monson of Auburn. From left to right are an Onondaga County sheriff's deputy, Carl Festa, another Onondaga County sheriff's deputy, and Carmen Bertonica.

From left to right are officers Charles Augello, Pete Killian, William Cadwallader, and Al Wilson. Cadwallader was promoted to sergeant on January 12, 1976. Today he is the department's training sergeant in charge of all training-related issues, including scheduling.

Officer Anthony D'Alberto points to evidence found in the road, probably during the midnight shift, as the streets appear to be empty of cars. D'Alberto was appointed patrolman on December 31, 1961. He resigned on August 9, 1975

Officers gather in the lineup room, in the basement at the police department. From left to right are Al Wilson, Alex Lepak, Don Quinn, Bernard Watkins, Sgt. John Walter, Ronald Semple, Tom Murphy, and Doug Parker. Still in use today, the lineup room was updated in the mid-1990s.

Officers Sam Emmi (left) and brother Steve Emmi pose together in the early 1970s. Notice the siren on top of the patrol car. Today OSHA requires that the siren be placed in the front grill area to reduce the noise level inside the police car.

Capt. Hugh Casey works at his desk. In 1969, a police captain made $7,845 a year and a sergeant made $7,132 a year. The patrol captain got his own office when the police garage was converted to office space.

The Volkswagen Beetle lost this battle. It ran into the back of a city bulldozer. This Volkswagen was car 8. Notice the police decal on the door. Today car 8 would be unit 418, the patrol supervisor's car.

Pres. Bill Clinton leaves the William H. Seward House during a visit to Auburn with his wife, Hillary Rodham Clinton. The Clintons spent time in Auburn during one summer vacation. During this stay they toured both the Seward house and the Harriet Tubman Home on South Street. Officer Tom Weed is on the far left.

Police investigate a fatal school bus–pedestrian car accident on North Street on February 14, 1978. The view was taken looking toward Seymour Street. Notice the price of gas at the Sunoco station (right): 58¢ a gallon.

This photograph was taken from a position on Market Street right next to the police station before urban renewal. Today the statue of Mayor Osborne is still in front of the station, facing North Street, but all of the buildings along North Street are gone.

This 1959 or 1960 black-and-white patrol car is parked on the corner of West Genesee Street and Delevan Street. Officer Steve Emmi is directing traffic behind the patrol car. The store in front of him is Doan's Market and Wilson's food store. Today that building is gone and the site serves as the parking lot for Rickey's restaurant.

Officers gather in the lineup room at the police department. From left to right are Carl Townsend, Myron Szul, Dom DeSocio, John Moochler (foreground), Mike Cicora, Sgt. Ray Wood (seated), Joe Fabrize, David Buckingham, Steve Emmi, Alex Lepak, and Eric Drisko.

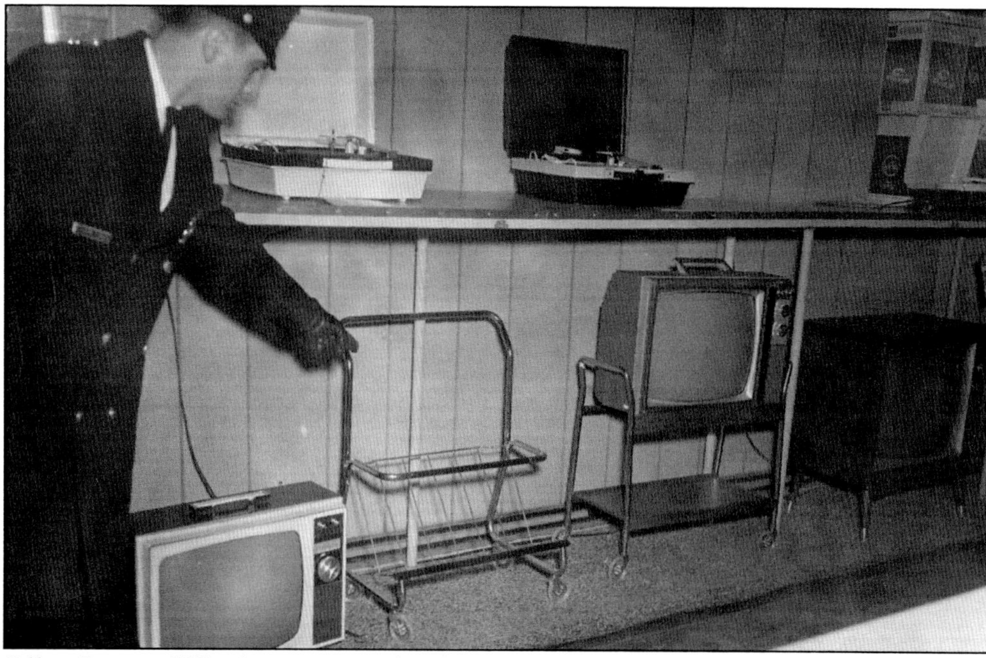

Officer Raymond Wood investigates a burglary at Peck's Radio and TV on Grant Avenue. Wood was appointed patrolman on June 20, 1960, was promoted to sergeant on August 12, 1971, was transferred to the detective bureau as a detective sergeant in April 1974, and was promoted to assistant chief of police on August 18, 1988.

Assistant police chief John Tenity (seated) was an Auburn School Board member from 1975 to 1979. Behind him are, from left to right, Capt. Wayne Armitage, detective Carl Festa, and two officials.

Sgt. Frank Colella (left) and officer Tony D'Alberto investigate a motor vehicle accident on South Street in front of the Harriet Tubman Home in the early 1970s. The Tubman home is behind the officers.

Pres. Ronald Reagan was in Auburn in 1979 campaigning before the Republican primary. Officer Doug Parker can be seen behind the president (upper left). Other officers in the photograph are John Costello, John Shwaryk, and Charlie Elser.

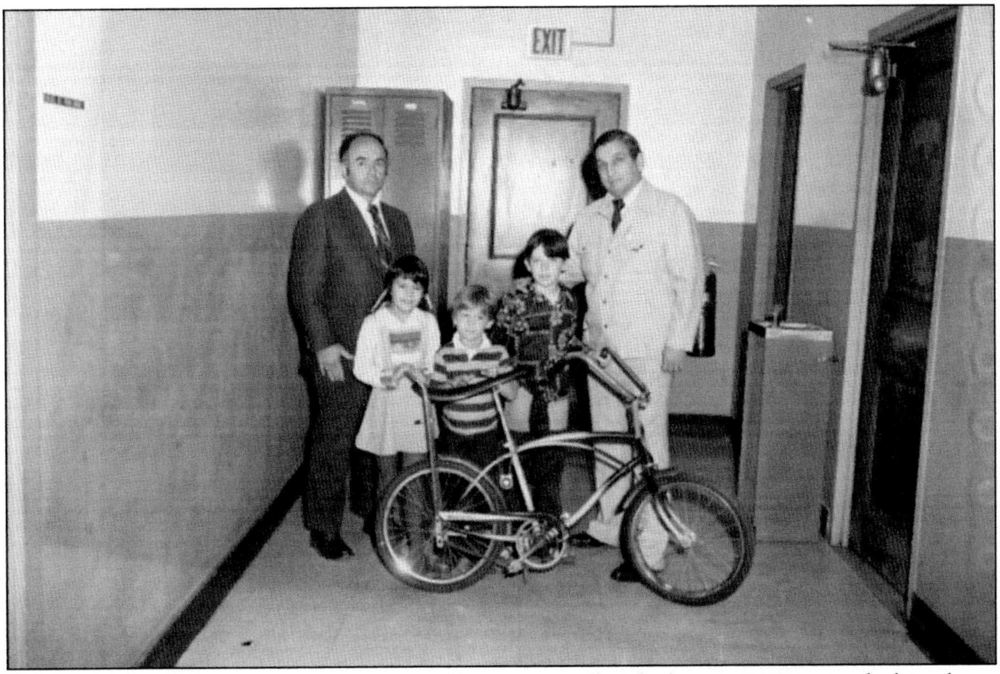

Detectives Carl Festa (left) and Jimmy Cioffa are pictured with three youngsters and a bicycle on the second floor of the police department. Today the Detective and Identification Bureaus are on the second floor. The wall behind Festa has been opened to make way for offices.

Officer Tom Burger glances at the camera while directing traffic downtown on South Street. Burger was appointed patrolman on May 18, 1969, and was promoted to detective, his current position, on April 13, 1997. Burger is the coauthor of the book *Auburn: Murder Stories*, published in 2007.

Officer Pat Shea is shown during his last night on patrol. On August 22, 1987, he was promoted to detective. Today he is the department's youth officer. He handles youth-related problems that need to be forwarded to family court.

Officer John Moochler is in the driver's seat of a 1976 Ford Torino at H&L Ford on Grant Avenue. Moochler was appointed patrolman on May 1, 1956. He retired on January 1, 1985.

Sen. Hillary Rodham Clinton shakes hands with detective Pat Shea, as Auburn fire chief Michael Quill (left) and others watch. The photograph was taken at the Harriet Tubman Home on South Street in Auburn.

Officer Myron Szul investigates an automobile accident on Owasco Street. Szul was appointed patrolman on May 21, 1979, and was promoted to detective in 1994. He became the department's first detective to handle exclusively domestic violence cases. He followed up on every domestic violence case initially investigated by patrol. He retired in 2002.

Capt. Wayne Armitage checks with the switchboard operators. Donna Napieracz (seated) started with the department on February 23, 1976, as a switchboard operator. Today she continues to work, part time, in the police records department. Audrey Hogan was hired as secretary to the chief of police on July 1, 1968. She retired in 1989.

Detective Tom Murphy (left) testifies at the Jimmy Lee Rouse murder trial. Rouse walked into Robbie's bar on Chapman Avenue and shot two men. One of the men died. Murphy was appointed patrolman on May 13, 1974, and was promoted to detective on November 9, 1988, to captain in charge of the detective bureau shortly thereafter, and to deputy chief under police chief Gary Giannotta in 2001.

Officers standing guard at the police line are, from left to right, John Shwaryk, James Bender, and Tony Ventura. They are outside 14 Frederick Street, the scene of a double murder-suicide on April 11, 1990. Allen Sessions killed Duane Whitaker and Tracy Clemens before committing suicide. Clemens's baby was left unharmed on the couch in the same room the murders took place.

From left to right are officers Dan McLaughlin, Al Wilson, Bernard Watkins, Alex Lepak, Sgt. John Loveland (seated), Charlie Elser, and Steve Emmi. Watkins was appointed patrolman on October 2, 1967, at the age of 23, and was promoted to sergeant in 1983, and to captain in 1985. Lepak was appointed on June 4, 1963, and was promoted to sergeant on March 8, 1981.

From left to right are officers Dan Colella, Carl Festa, Pete Killian, and Jack Malone. Colella, who retired in 1991, was appointed on December 15, 1969. Killian, who retired in 1992, was appointed patrolman on July 1, 1957. He served as the police union president for 25 years.

Officer Ron Nagell investigates an automobile accident involving the police department's "Stop DWI" patrol car. At the time of this accident, officer Edward Fabrize had a car pulled over and was in the process of making a DWI arrest when the car shown on the left stuck the patrol car. The driver in the second car was also charged with DWI.

Officers and brothers Dan DeMaio (left) and Joe DeMaio served on the force together for over 20 years. Dan was appointed on December 5, 1955, and Joe was appointed on June 7, 1954, by city manager Alfred Turner. Dan retired on January 1, 1978, and Joe retired six months earlier, on July 1, 1977.

Capt. Tom Piscotti stands by his unmarked patrol car on Dunning Avenue. Someone threw a rock at the patrol car, breaking the rear window. Piscotti and Bernard Watkins were promoted to captain at the same time. Filling the two sergeant slots were officers Robert Carberry and Alan Wilson.

The police department conducts a bicycle registration program. Bicycles brought to the station are issued a sticker. If the bicycle gets lost or stolen and (with sticker intact) is later recovered by the department, it can be returned to its owner. Here officer Vito Tozzi registers a bicycle for its owner.

Detective Carmen Bertonica points to damage on a car. In 1974, Bertonica was promoted to captain and reassigned to the patrol division. Sgt. Ray Wood took Bertonica's place in the detective bureau, and John Walter was promoted to sergeant, filling the vacancy left by Wood. The promotions and transfers were made by Chief John Costello.

Thousands of protesters show up to express their opposition to the neo-Nazis who came to march in Auburn in 1993. Police departments from around central New York assisted Auburn in preparing for the march. The march started at city hall. Notice the patrol car. All of its windows were taped to prevent flying glass in the event of broken windows.

During the neo-Nazi march of 1993, an anti-Nazi protester crosses the police line in an attempt to be heard. Notice the jacket the man is carrying. The officer escorted the man back behind the lines without a problem.

Crowds gather around a patrol car as the neo-Nazi's prepare to march from city hall down South Street. Notice the police in riot gear coming up the rear.

Officer Charlie Elser is getting in a Dodge Diplomat patrol car in the 1980s. The dark blue Dodge (background) is the "old look." The cars with the new look are white with a blue stripe.

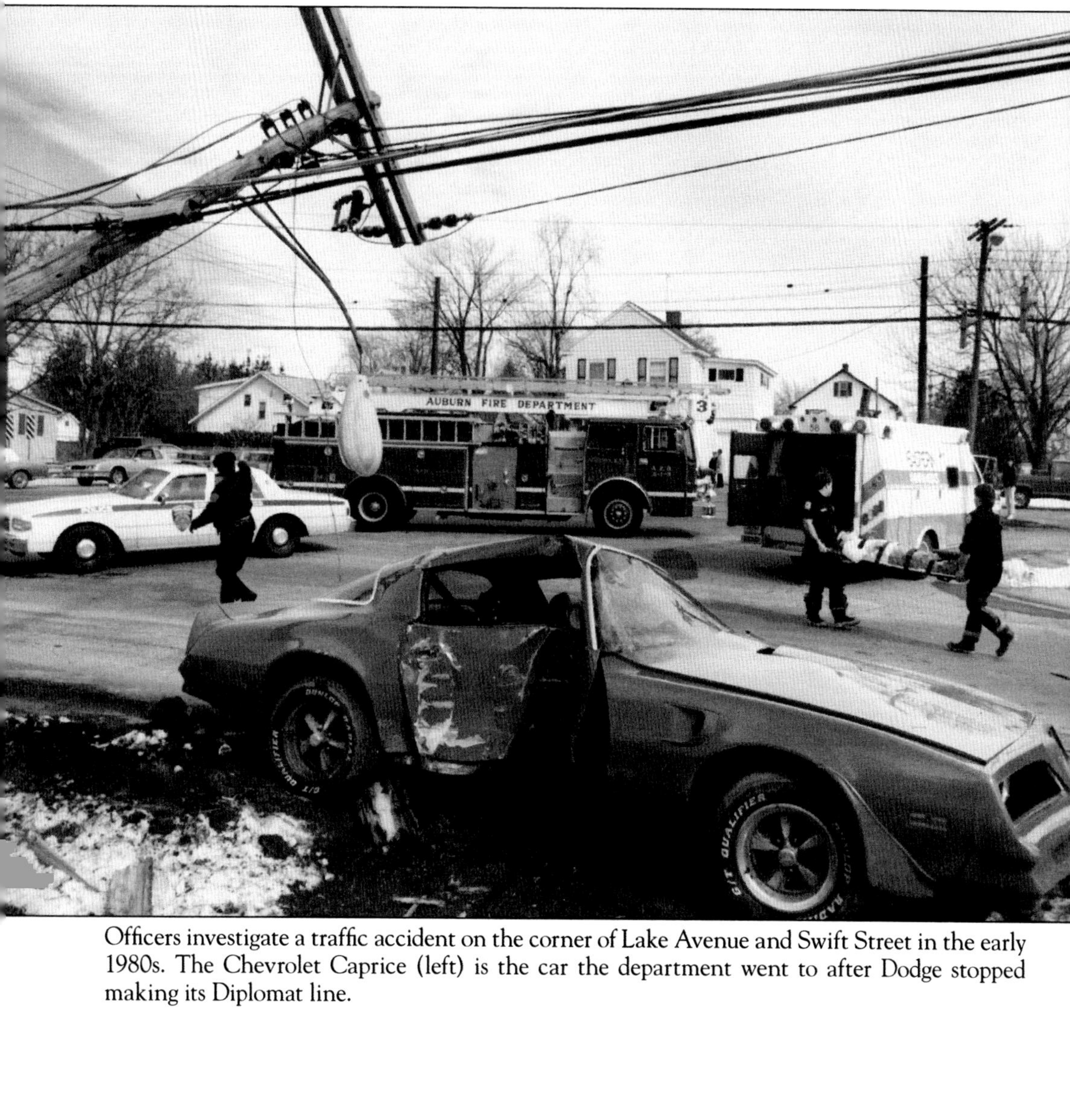

Officers investigate a traffic accident on the corner of Lake Avenue and Swift Street in the early 1980s. The Chevrolet Caprice (left) is the car the department went to after Dodge stopped making its Diplomat line.

Officer Steve Emmi poses with three Dodge Diplomats in the parking lot at the police department. The Diplomat was the car used by almost every police department in the 1980s. Dodge stopped making the car in the late 1980s.

Before individual desks were brought in, a large table was used for police meetings. This meeting is being held in the lineup room. From left to right are officers Joe DeMaio, Pete Aversa, Sam Emmi, Sgt. Frank Colella, Dom DeSocio, Steve Emmi, and Joe Fabrize.

Officer Gary Giannotta investigates a traffic accident on Genesee Street next to Whitings Paint and Wallpaper. Giannotta went on to become chief of police. Whitings is no longer on Genesee Street, it moved to a newer building on Fulton Street. The streetlights have been replaced by more traditional downtown lampposts.

From left to right are officers Ray Wood, John Walter, Dave Buckingham, and Ron Bent. Buckingham, who joined the force on May 18, 1969, was promoted to sergeant in 1988—on the same day that Tom Burger, Eric Drisko, and Gary Giannotta were promoted to sergeant.

Two officers are at the scene of the Kenneth Lafever homicide in 1989: detective Mike Pitcher (left) and Don Gosline. Gosline was promoted to sergeant in June 1996.

Officer Steve Emmi (left) and Sgt. Dave Buckingham are at Holland Stadium getting ready for an Auburn High School varsity football game. Emmi was appointed on February 26, 1961.

Officer Ronald Nagell sits in the lineup room. This is the newest lineup room in use today. Every officer reporting for duty starts the workday in this room. From here the sergeant gives out assignments and passes on any pertinent information for the shift ahead. Nagell was appointed on December 7, 1967. He was an EMT and evidence technician. He retired in 1997.

Sgt. Ray Wood celebrates a birthday. Wood made his way through the ranks to assistant chief. When police chief John Walter retired, Wood was named acting chief until John Ecklund was named permanent chief of police.

Outside with their patrol cars are, from left to right, officers Paul Casper, Doug Parker, and Frank Lumb. Parker was appointed on May 15, 1972, and was promoted to detective on December 31, 1990. Lumb was appointed patrolman on October 18, 1976.

An unruly person is arrested at the scene of a fire. Officers handling the situation are, from left to right, Steve Montgomery, Gregory Shwaryk, and Brian Clancy.

Identification officer William Simmonds checks for latent fingerprints on a stolen car. This photograph was taken in the police garage by detective Longo on April 29, 1964.

A new black-and-white patrol car is parked in the park in front of the police department under the statue of Mayor Thomas Osborne. In the late 1990s, the department went to this design, and today's police cars still have this paint design, with only a few modifications in the lettering. The look was popular with other law enforcement agencies, many of which later changed their cars to black-and-whites. Officer Tom Weed took this photograph.

Three police cars are parked at Hoopes Park. From left to right are a patrol car; a Pontiac sports car, seized by the department from a drug dealer and converted for use in the DARE (Drug Abuse Resistance Education) program; and a "Stop DWI" car, assigned to an officer responsible only for traffic enforcement. Detective Sgt. James Bender took this photograph.

At the police department's indoor firing range, Tom Murphy stands behind Myron Szul. In the late 1960s, the league competition was held in this room. The state police pistol team came in first place, edging out Auburn in the winter pistol league. The Outcasts team, representing Auburn Correctional Facility, placed third.

Officer Tom Weed (left) receives a commendation from police chief James Moochler for saving and performing CPR on a baby who fell into a toilet. The baby resumed breathing but unfortunately did not live long. Moochler, who served as intern chief after John Ecklund resigned, spend 30 years with the state police before retiring at the rank of major.

Taking inventory of seized bags of marijuana are, from left to right, detectives Tom Piscotti, John Malandruccolo, and Carl Festa. At this time, Piscotti was assigned to the district attorney's office as confidential investigator under district attorney Pete Corning.

The police department went to this design in the mid-1990s. Chief Tom Piscotti wanted the cars to have "community service" written on them. This design only lasted two years before being replaced with a different look.

This car was the design of police cars in the early 1990s. The brand-new supervisor's car 418 sits at the county motor pool on York Street. At the time, the city had a contract with the county to service all of the city police cars. Today the patrol cars are serviced by city mechanics at the central garage on West Genesee Street.

From left to right are David Buckingham, Ron Bent, Harold "Red" Quinn, and Tom Piscotti. Quinn and Piscotti were assigned to the district attorney's office under district attorney Peter Corning. Today the district attorney's office has its own investigator.

Officers qualify with their service weapons under Tom Murphy (second from right), range officer. With Murphy are, from left to right, Don Quinn, Dan Colella, Phil Stanton, and Tom Burger, holding the shotgun. Quinn was appointed patrolman on May 24, 1963. Stanton was appointed on August 20, 1969. He retired in 1991.

Car 431 was the "Stop DWI" car around 2000. It never had overhead emergency lights. Its emergency lights were in the front and back windows. This car was paid for by the Cayuga County Stop DWI Committee. Today the committee no longer pays for a car, but the city still funds the program, allowing a full-time Stop DWI patrol.

A train crossing State Street derailed, and two boxcars fell into the Owasco Outlet in 2003. No one was injured. Lt. James Bender (left) confers with detective Doug Parker on the bridge next to the prison on State Street. Bender was appointed on February 18, 1985, and was promoted to detective in 1993, detective sergeant in 1996, and lieutenant in charge of the detective bureau in 2001.

Husband and wife Megan and Andy Kalet are shown in 2004. Megan is one of seven evidence technicians who are responsible for processing crime scenes. Andy is one of the department's K-9 officers. The department has two K-9 units assigned to patrol.

Officer Joseph DiVietro is shown with his daughter, Allison, in 2001. DiVietro was appointed to the department on September 19, 1990, reassigned to the identification bureau in 2001, and promoted to sergeant in charge of the identification bureau in 2005.

Officers pose outside the police department in 2002. Seen here are (first row) Meghan Kalet, Gary Giannotta, Tom Murphy, Dan Emmi, and James Bender; (second row) Tom Weed, Mark LoCastro, Stephan McLoughlin, Charles Augello, Greg Guilfus, Sean Butler, Dan McLoughlin, Joe Villano, Bill Cadwallader, Donald Gosline, Tom Burger, Myron Szul, and Dave Buckingham.

Officers protest at city hall in 2005 in response to a threat to lay off 10 patrolmen. The signs say, "How long do you want to wait for help?" and "Say no to laying off police officers." In the end no officer was laid off. Among those pictured are (front to back) James Bender, William Gleason, Angelo Spinelli, Gregory Dann, Stephan Mcloughlin, Shawn Daly, Mark Schattinger, Mike Roden, and Doug Parker.

John Breeze (left) smiles at his graduation from the police academy in 2000. With him is his grandfather Carmen Bertonica, who was appointed patrolman on July 3, 1953, and was promoted to sergeant on May 1, 1968, to captain in March 1974, and to assistant police chief on December 9, 1979.

Sgt. Robert Carberry sits in the command center. Carberry was promoted to sergeant on February 1, 1985. He and Al Wilson were promoted at the same time to fill vacancies left by the promotions to captain of Tom Piscotti and Bernard Watkins.

From left to right are officers Chris Major, Brian Blanchfield, Tom Weed, and Jimmy Slayton. The photograph was taken in 2005. Major and Slayton are currently assigned to the Auburn School District as school resource officers.

Sgt. Brian Clancy sits at the command center. Clancy was appointed on May 1, 1985, and was promoted to sergeant on July 23, 1995. The command center, or sergeant's desk, is manned 24 hours a day, seven days a week. At one time a telephone operator and dispatcher worked in this area. Today all calls into the police department are answered by the 911 center on County House Road.

Pictured in the command center are Paul Casper (left) and Angelo Spinelli. Casper was appointed on April 11, 1988, and was promoted to detective on January 4, 1999. This area was formerly the police building's three-car garage.

Stephan McLoughlin stands with his father, Sgt. Dan Mcloughlin. The father was appointed to the department on December 17, 1973, and the son on July 24, 2000. Both are wearing dress uniforms. The department went back to the dress uniform in the late 1990s.

Officers are pictured in full-dress uniform in front of the police department in 2004. They are, from left to right, (first row) Lt. Dan Emmi and detective Tom Burger; (second row) Sgt. Don Gosline, Mike Roden, and Capt. David Delfavero.

This photograph was taken at the funeral of police chief John Costello. The funeral was held at Holy Family Church on North Street. From left to right are Ron Bent, Bob Orman, Donald Quinn, John Sawran, Skaneateles police chief O'Neil, Tom Burger, Chris Major, Tom Weed, Jeff Mead, Doug Parker, Gary Giannotta, Charles Augello, Dan Mcloughlin, Dan Emmi, Bill Cadwallader, James Bender, David Buckingham, and Pat Shea.

From left to right are detectives Pat Shea, Jeff Mead, Tom Burger, and Doug Parker, Lt. James Bender (seated), and Sgt. Joseph DiVietro. Bender retired in 2007, the year this picture was taken. This office is located on the second floor. In the late 1930s, it was the locker room and the Detective Bureau was located in the basement.

Pictured outside are Joe Villlano, Mark Locastro, Megan Kalet, Capt. Charles Augello, Andy Kalet, Shawn Butler, Sgt. William Cadwallader, and Mike Roden.

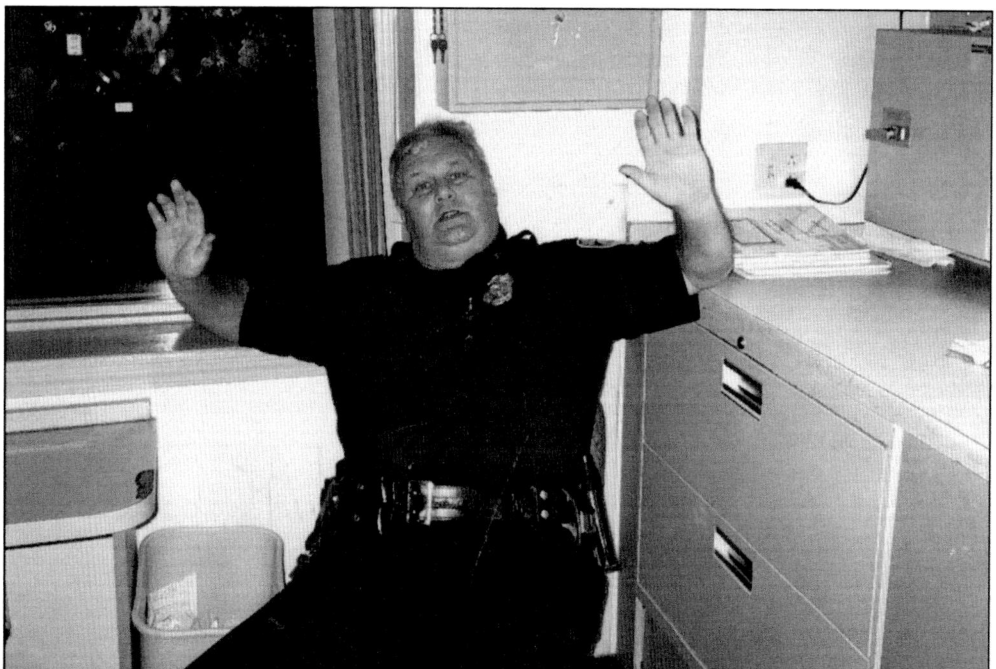

Officer Greg Shwaryk strikes his best pose. "The Commander," as he was called, was appointed to the department on May 15, 1972. He retired in 2005, and today he is an assistant coroner's investigator for the Cayuga County Coroner's Office.

Three

Police Headquarters

The original city hall housed the police department, city hall employees, and a food market in the basement. The building was located on North Street on the site where the police department stands today.

This is the brand-new police and fire departments at 46 North Street in 1931. It took about one year to construct the building. The plans were made by architects Coolidge, Shepley, Bulfinch and Abbott, the same firm that designed the new city hall on South Street. The new building is 7,674 square feet.

This 1930s photograph is looking down Market Street toward North Street. The fire chief's office has not been built yet. The new building cost $325,000, the entire city council led by Mayor Charles Osborne agreed the police needed a new and modern building. The station was built with an indoor shooting range.

This early-1940s view is on North Street looking toward Genesee Street. The weather vane on top of the building is no longer there; it sits in storage in the attic of the department. The church on the left fell down in the mid-1970s.

This is one of the few photographs showing the word "Police" above the door. The door was the main entrance to the department until the garage was converted to offices. Today this door is rarely used. To right of the door on the ground is a grave marker for Pal, the department dog.

This is how the police department looks today. The three-car garage is gone, replaced by offices. The photograph was taken on November 16, 2001, just after the parking lot was paved. The slate roof was replaced in 2002.

MAP SEARCH